Witt

For all its buzzing café culture, the boho neighbourhood of Cihangir has always lacked decent guest accommodation. That changed in 2008 when the owner of the Witt hotel, Tuncel Toprak, spotted this corner lot with classic views towards the minarets of Sultanahmet and the Bosphorus. Today, this is the hotel of choice for visiting art-world and fashion folk, who can sink into the stylish lobby (above) and one of the 17 suites, all designed by Autoban, while taking in the cool air blowing in from the strait. The views from the Penthouse Suite make it one of the best rooms in town. Otherwise, opt for a City View Suite (overleaf). *Defterdar Yokusu 26, T 212 293 1500, www.wittistanbul.com*

City View Suite, Witt

Four Seasons Hotel Bosphorus
The Four Seasons on the Bosphorus, opened in 2008, quickly became the preferred location for the visiting élite. Like many of the other Bosphorus hotels, this is a rebuilt version of an Ottoman *yalı*, with additions such as the huge front terrace and pool area. The indoor pool (opposite) is the most tranquil retreat. Service is impeccable, as you'd expect at a Four Seasons, and the guest rooms, such as the Palace Bosphorous Room (above), are airy and well appointed. For guests and visitors, the expansive spa on the ground floor offers the pain and pleasure of fully equipped men's and women's Turkish hammams. If you want to be close to the main sights, check into the Four Seasons in Sultanahmet, which is housed in a neoclassical former prison. The rooftop terrace offers a brilliant vista.
Çırağan Caddesi 28, T 212 381 4000
www.fourseasons.com/bosphorus

A'jia

Globetrotters and brothers Levent, Riza and Bülent Büyükuğur have a knack for importing international design concepts and reinterpreting them into their own Turkish treats. This time, the owners of the acclaimed Istanbul Doors Restaurant Group transformed a handsome 17th-century mansion into a luxurious boutique hotel. Perched on the edge of the water in Kanlıca, the A'jia offers 16 modern, clean-lined rooms, such as the Bosphorous Pasha Room (left), with views over the water. Among A'jia's excellent amenities are a speed boat shuttle service to and from the European side of the city. The in-house Mediterranean restaurant has a particularly good reputation.

Çubuklu Caddesi 27, T 216 413 9300, www.ajiahotel.com

W

With its high hip quotient, the W boasts a blatant East-meets-West interior, which serves as the backdrop to the hotel's lively social scene. The building was the centrepiece renovation of the Akaretler row houses in Beşiktaş and the location is ideal. Stroll along to art galleries Galerist (T 212 244 8230) and Rampa (T 212 327 0800), and the design shops Autoban Gallery Akaretler (T 212 236 9246) and Derin (see p073), stopping for lunch at Corvus Wine & Bite (see p048). Nearby attractions include Dolmabahçe Palace. Rooms, such as the Wow Suite (opposite and above), have wide terraces providing a welcome sense of space in this dense part of town. Settle in to the first-floor lounge for some prime people-watching.
Süleyman Seba Caddesi 22, T 212 381 2121, www.wistanbul.com.tr

Sumahan on the Water

Not so long ago, the Asian side of the Bosphorus wasn't an obvious spot for one of Istanbul's most successful design-led hotels. But that's where Sumahan on the Water opened in a 19th-century former drinks factory. Each of the hotel's 18 rooms, all stylishly furnished like the Executive Suite (above), offers magical views of the city's minaret skyline. With its private boat, top-flight fish restaurant, Kordon, and luxurious Turkish hammam, Sumahan has made Çengelköy a new hotel hotspot. To get a taste of old Istanbul, explore the adjacent area of Üsküdar. *Kuleli Caddesi 51, T 216 422 8000, www.sumahan.com*

The House Hotel Nişantaşı

The House chain of hotels is expanding
across the city as quickly as The House
Cafés did a few years back. With locations
in Galatasaray, Nişantaşı and Ortaköy,
they are a step up from their café cousins
in terms of luxury. We've chosen the
Nişantaşı property for its proximity to
the city's tony shopping district (the hotel
is situated above the Prada store), and
because it is perhaps Autoban's sleekest
interior design effort for the group. The
tone is sophisticated, with wood and
leather furniture, marble bathrooms and
subdued lighting, from the lobby/lounge
(above) to the cosy rooms; we opted for a
Terrace Deluxe Room (opposite). It all feels
miles away from the din outside. If it's
Bosphorous views you crave, check in to
the Ortaköy hotel (T 212 244 3400), set in
a restored 19th-century landmark building.
*Abdi Ipekci Caddesi 34, T 212 224 5999,
www.thehousehotel.com*

The Sofa Hotel

Spitting distance from the Istanbul Convention and Exhibition Centre (T 212 296 3055), The Sofa bridges the gap between business- and design-led hotel. The ugly exterior belies a contemporary interior with an artsy edge. There's a bookstore on the first floor, which sells international magazines and newspapers; an in-house restaurant, Supermarket by Longtable, which attracts on-the-scene locals; and an art gallery with a terrace that can be hired for private functions. All 82 rooms have wi-fi access and a '24hr Anything Anytime Button'. If you are in the city on business, we recommend the Executive Suite (pictured), with its generous living-room area. The shopping hub of Nişantaşı is steps away.
Teşvikiye Caddesi 41, T 212 368 1818, www.thesofahotel.com

24 HOURS
SEE THE BEST OF THE CITY IN JUST ONE DAY

Not every city can offer the geographic coup of skipping from one continent to another. So a day zigzagging the Bosphorus, because you can, is a great thing to do. We've assumed you are staying in or near Sultanahmet, the city's historic heart. Whether you're a first-time visitor or a Constantinople pro, start the day with a dervish-style spin in Sultanahmet Square, to drink in the wraparound views of Aya Sofya (Aya Sofya Meydanı, T 212 522 1750) and the Blue Mosque (Sultanahmet Parkı, T 212 518 1319). From here, it's a short walk to Yerebatan Sarnıcı (opposite), the underground cisterns, then on to the Eminönü waterfront where you can catch a ferry or cross the bridge to Galata. In this area, we recommend a visit to the Autoban Gallery (see p034), stopping for lunch afterwards at the Istanbul Modern (see p035) in Karaköy.

In the afternoon, make your way up the coast for a tour around the stunning Dolmabahçe Palace (see p036), then hop on a ferry over to Asia to have tea in one of Üsküdar's many cafés. It's best to bypass the bridges and take the boat back to Europe, continuing up the coast for an alfresco aperitif at The House Café Ortaköy (Salhane Sokak 1, T 212 227 2699). Head back downtown for dinner at the cosmopolitan Changa (see p037) near Taksim Square. For those who want to party on, the 11:11 nightclub (see p038) is a hotspot for late-night dancing and drinks.

For full addresses, see Resources.

10.00 Yerebatan Sarnıcı

As many as 60 underground cisterns were built to irrigate the gardens of Byzantine Constantinople, the largest of which is the Sunken Palace, or Yerebatan Sarayı. Covering more than 9,712 sq m, this is one of the city's most evocative sights, featuring a forest of 336 marble columns (through which James Bond rowed a boat in *From Russia With Love*). Just a stone's throw west of Aya Sofya, it provides cool respite on a hot summer's day. Ignore the coloured lights, piped-in music and gift shop; instead concentrate on the spooky acoustics, algae-covered columns and the ghostly fish that swim beneath your feet.
Yerebatan Caddesi 13, T 212 522 1259, www.yerebatan.com

11.30 Autoban Gallery

Autoban and modern design in Istanbul have, for several years, been synonymous, thanks to the furniture and lighting produced in the design studio's workshops in the historic section of Galata. The brand's prolific young design duo, Seyhan Özdemir and Sefer Çağlar, were initially responsible for a series of restaurant interiors, starting with the now ubiquitous House Café and Kitchenette chains, which defined a new type of lifestyle space for the city. Despite the fact that Autoban's partnership with high-end furnishing company De La Espada has resulted in some of the production shifting to Portugal, many of the firm's covetable chairs, sofas, tables, shelves and lights are still made by local craftsmen in Galata. *Meşrutiyet Caddesi 64a, T 212 252 6797, www.autoban212.com*

13.00 Istanbul Modern

If ever a building had an agenda, it's this one. As well as being Turkey's first national museum of contemporary art, it's also a symbol of the country's international outlook. The 8,000 sq m gallery is located in Karaköy in an ex-naval warehouse. It opened in 2004 and is dedicated to promoting Turkish art. Alongside its permanent collection, it hosts exhibitions and individual works by international artists, such as Richard Wentworth's *False Ceiling* (above). There's also an auditorium, video-art gallery and new-media centre. From the second floor, there are great views across the peninsula. The café/restaurant (T 212 292 2612) is an ideal spot for lunch, especially if you snag a seat on the terrace.
Meclis-i Mebusan Caddesi, T 212 334 7300, www.istanbulmodern.org

15.00 Dolmabahçe Palace

If you only have time to take in one palace, make sure it's this large slice of Bosphorus baroque, which was home to the Ottoman sultans from 1856. It must have strained their treasury almost as much as it did Atatürk – he died in the palace in 1938 in a seaside room that has been untouched ever since. The Sèvres-stuffed interior, by Charles Séchan, designer of the Opéra in Paris, consists of 285 rooms, six hammams and VIP quarters for harems and the chief eunuch. It also boasts the largest chandelier in the world, which weighs in at an impressive 4.5 tonnes.
Dolmabahçe Caddesi, T 212 236 9000, www.dolmabahcepalace.com

20.00 Changa

This was a groundbreaking restaurant for Istanbul when it opened in 1999. It presented one of Turkey's first 'fusion' menus, created by the New Zealand-born chef Peter Gordon. Turkish ingredients were melded with Pacific and Asian flavours in elegantly styled dishes that drew locals and visitors alike. Today, it still rates highly for its food and lively bar scene, offering some of the city's most creative cocktails, such as a fragrant raki, vodka and tangerine combination called an Istanbul. With its contemporary interior set within a townhouse off Taksim Square, Changa has evolved into a classic eaterie. Perhaps it's only now that the city is truly beginning to understand its nuances and sophistication.
Sıraselviler Caddesi 47, T 212 251 7064, www.changa-istanbul.com

23.00 11:11
One of the few late-night dance venues
in Istanbul, 11:11 has all the clubbing
essentials: burly doormen, dramatic
lighting and a full-on sound system.
Its geometric, cave-like interior makes
it one of the most eye-catching clubs
in town. DJs on the international circuit
arrive to spin techno and deep house.
Meşrutiyet Caddesi 69, T 212 244 8834,
www.1111.com.tr

URBAN LIFE
CAFÉS, RESTAURANTS, BARS AND NIGHTCLUBS

Partly because this is such a mighty metropolis (with its sheer scale, brio and 212 phone code, Istanbul sees itself as a Balkan Big Apple), and partly because of its seasonal patterns and the hunger of its denizens for novelty, venues tend to fall out of favour here with bewildering speed. An additional problem in choosing places to frequent is the sponsorship that creeps into many bars, clubs and even restaurants. While we can forgive a cigarette branded lampshade or two, it's a shame to see an otherwise decent venue marred by an interior design based on Johnnie Walker bottles or billboards advertising 4x4s.

In summer, do as the locals do and scope out the venues with a terrace and a view, such as Anjelique (Muallim Naci Caddesi Salhane Sokak 5, T 212 327 2844). Depending on your preference you can get down and dirty in the myriad bars, restaurants and clubs, such as the late-night DJ bar Mini Müzikhol (Sıraselviler Caddesi, Soğancı Sokak 7), near Istiklâl Caddesi – the busy thoroughfare that links Tünel and Taksim – or head for the more scenic, serene and less touristy (but further afield) spots along the Bosphorus in hugely popular Bebek or Kuruçeşme. A much touted treat is the chance to dine in Asia with the minimum of fuss. The formerly down-at-heel Üsküdar neighbourhood is now brimming with excellent seafood restaurants.

For full addresses, see Resources.

Köşebaşı

While many other cultures 'do' kebab, it's the Turks who have brought it into the 21st century with style. At the head of this movement is Köşebaşı, an Istanbul institution now boasting 11 branches in Turkey and six international locations, as far afield as São Paulo. This expansion has not lessened the experience at the original location, which has hardly changed since it opened in 1995. The long, sizzling grill of kebabs on spits still greets visitors as they enter a room buzzing with Turkish families and office workers from the Levent and Maslak business districts. Köşebaşı's kebab, originating from south-eastern Turkey, features the mini-cubed çöp şiş and side dishes such as tangy diced tomato salad in pomegranate juice.
Çamlık Sokak 15, T 212 270 2433, www.kosebasi.com

Dükkan Steakhouse

Turks like their meat. From kebab to *köfte* meatballs, they will go the extra mile to find the best – even if that means ending up in Armutlu, one of Istanbul's many squatter districts. Butcher-turned-restaurateur Emre Mermer set up a wholesale cold-storage depot here because of its central location, but quickly decided to turn his warehouse into a butcher's shop. The increasing popularity of his locally sourced beef and lamb in turn prompted the entrepreneur to transform Dükkan into a steakhouse, which today attracts connoisseurs for its mix of air-dried and fresh cuts. The grill in the middle of the intimate dining area is never allowed to cool, and anchors a room that has sweeping views of the surreal squatter and skyscraper skyline. *Atatürk Caddesi 6, T 212 277 8860, www.dukkanistanbul.com*

Vogue

Now more than a decade old, Vogue has become an Istanbul classic – not surprising when you learn that it's run by the Istanbul Doors Restaurant Group, the company behind many of the city's coolest bars, hotels (see p022) and restaurants. The menu is refreshed at an almost alarming rate but the food is always spot on, and the sushi bar is one of the best in town. Plant yourself on the 13th-floor terrace (above) of the Beşiktaş Plaza building and enjoy a late-afternoon drink and a sweeping early-evening view of the Bosphorus and the old city. *BJK Plaza, Spor Caddesi, T 212 227 4404, www.istanbuldoors.com*

Mangerie

The upmarket district of Bebek on the Bosphorus brims with cafés full of ladies who lunch. Mangerie, tucked away on the upper floor of an otherwise drab building in the centre of the area, is undoubtedly the best of the bunch. Head chef Elif Yalin has taken the formula behind her first venture, the hugely popular House Café chain, and upped the ante for both the cuisine and the ambience. The bright and breezy dining room and wide terrace offer stellar views over the water as diners dig in to Yalin's hearty, healthy fare prepared using local ingredients. We highly recommend the fish bread, which is exactly that, a grilled fish fillet in cornbread – a variant of an Istanbul street-food favourite.
Cevdet Paşa Caddesi 69, T 212 263 5199, www.mangeriebebek.com

Delicatessen
Rows of cheese, cold meats, bread and
olives greet guests at this shop/eaterie
run by Istanbul's slow-food maestro Elif
Yalin of Mangerie (see p045). Upstairs
is dominated by the bar (pictured);
downstairs offers proper dining.
The wine list is long, with many labels
available by the glass, a rarity in Istanbul.
*Mim Kemal Öke Caddesi 19/1, T 212 225
0607, www.delicatessenistanbul.com*

Corvus Wine & Bite

Corvus, one of Turkey's new generation of high-quality vineyards, has brought the flavours of the nearby Northern Aegean to a central location in the restored Akaretler row houses of Beşiktaş. A no-reservations policy at its popular Corvus Wine & Bite means getting to dinner early (six o'clock) by Istanbul standards. Once seated, choose from Corvus' award-winning collection of wines and one of the many small plates of vegetables, cheese and seafood based on ingredients from the label's homeland – Bozcaada, an island in the Aegean with a long history of winemaking. Like the way your bottle of Corvus Corpus 2007 went with the Mediterranean greens? You can take it home with you, as the restaurant doubles as a shop for Corvus wines.
Şair Nedim Caddesi 5, T 212 260 5470

Ulus 29

The semicircular terrace of the eaterie Ulus 29 hovers over the Bosphorus and is a top spot in summer. Owned by Metin Fadıllıoğlu and his interior designer wife, Zeynep, who also designed the Beymen Brasserie (T 212 343 0443), the restaurant is a sumptuous mix of East-meets-West design and cuisine. The 29 in the name refers to the 29 traditional Ottoman and East Mediterranean dishes on the menu.

Turkish, French and Japanese chefs prepare the food, and recently introduced sushi dishes and an expansive cocktail list keep the locals coming.
Ahmet Adnan Saygun Caddesi, Ulus Parkı İçi 1, T 212 358 2929, www.club29.com

Müzedechanga

In 2005, six years after opening Changa (see p037), restaurateurs Tarik Bayazit and Savaş Ertunç opened this equally slick sequel. Their aim was to cater to the culture set flocking to the extended Sakıp Sabancı Müzesi (T 212 277 2200); the restaurant's name means 'Changa at the museum'. Architect Ayşen Savaş conceived the glass-cube structure that houses the restaurant; the retro-edged interiors were designed by Autoban, which chose Poul Henningsen and Noguchi lamps to bathe the eatery in light. Peter Gordon was put in charge of the food and offers his interpretation of traditional Turkish cuisine in dishes such as the house special Changa sucuk – a spicy local sausage with pistachios.
Sakıp Sabancı Caddesi 42, T 212 323 0901, www.changa-istanbul.com

Balikçi Sabahattin

A teeming labyrinth of sights and sounds during the day, Sultanahmet can become depressing in the evening, especially if you're looking for a good meal in a non-touristy setting. Providing one of the few decent dining options here is the Balikçi Sabahattin fish restaurant, located in a refurbished Ottoman townhouse within walking distance of the major landmarks. Alfresco dining in the little cobblestone piazza in front of the restaurant is very popular, so make sure you book ahead, especially in summer. Bypass the menu and go to inspect the fish yourself or, if you're lucky, the portly Sabahattin himself will wheel over the catch of the day, along with some of the finest mezze appetisers in town.
Seyit Hasan Kuyu 1, Cankurtaran,
T 212 458 1824, www.balikcisabahattin.com

Journey Lounge

Cihangir is a small, bohemian district
that draws creative types to its collection
of restaurants and bars. Day and night,
a clientele of local and international actors,
writers, designers and artists can be seen
whiling away their time in the cafés lining
the district's main street, Akarsu Caddesi.
Of these, Journey Lounge is the highlight,
for its airy interior and attention to design
detail. In the spirit of its location, the menu
and kitchen, managed by longtime
Istanbul restaurant professional Fisun
Taşgın, brings together regional Turkish
and global flavours in a very Cihangir
style, from breakfast to late.
Akarsu Caddesi 21a, T 212 244 8989

Ottosantral
Off the beaten path in the upper reaches
of the Golden Horn, Ottosantral – a
light-filled restaurant and event space
on the Santralistanbul campus of Bilgi
University (see p065) – is worth a visit
for its honest food and hip late-night
bar scene, which has a vibe that's more
East Village NYC than east Istanbul.
Santralistanbul, Kazım Karabekir
Caddesi 1, T 212 427 8068
www.ottoistanbul.com

Lokanta Maya
Since its 2009 launch, on a nondescript
street behind Istanbul's passenger ship
terminal, Lokanta Maya has served a
fusion of Mediterranean and Aegean
food. Chef and owner Didem Şenol has
written extensively on both subjects,
and it shows. She weaves seasonal
ingredients into fresh seafood which
she handpicks from local markets.
Kemankeş Caddesi 35, T 212 252 6884

Mikla

Istanbulites like taking their drinks with a view, and when a design-led, Schrager-esque setting is involved, it's bound to be a winner of a watering hole. Mikla, at the top of The Marmara Pera hotel (T 212 251 4646), is a haunt for the city's cool crowd. Its Eurocentric menu and minimal aesthetic conjure up a rather generic big-city atmosphere in the restaurant, but the floor-to-ceiling glass bar is hard to beat.

The small roof terrace with a pool adds an extra dimension. Settle with a cocktail and play spot the mosque. *The Marmara Pera, Meşrutiyet Caddesi 15, T 212 293 5656, www.miklarestaurant.com*

Lucca

For years, the upscale residential district of Bebek lacked anywhere to go beyond the dour Bebek Hotel and some fish restaurants. That all changed with the opening of a spate of new cafés and restaurants, Lucca being the undeniable leader of the pack. By day, it's the spot to mingle with Bebek's hip café society; by night, things ratchet up a notch, as a constant flow of sports cars and 4x4s bring a beautiful crowd of celebutantes, models and media personalities for a bar scene that lasts well into the night. Good food – bistro classics, plus a daily Turkish special – polished service and slick bartending guarantee a good, and often rather lively, time.

Cevdetpasa Caddesi 51b, T 212 257 1255

Münferit

Münferit's discreet setting behind the Galatasaray Lycée opens to an immaculate supperclub interior of white tablecloths and wood-panelled walls, created by Autoban. The breezy terraces make this a top spot for alfresco summer mezze, never more so than when the owner DJs in the upstairs cocktail lounge. *Yeni Çarşı Caddesi 19, T 212 252 5067, www.munferit.com.tr*

INSIDER'S GUIDE

MERVE ÇAĞLAR, GALLERY DIRECTOR

Originally from Izmir, Turkey's third largest city, Merve Çağlar runs the art space Galerist (Istiklal Caddesi 4, T 212 244 8230). Her life revolves around Beyoğlu, home to the city's artistic and creative community, and other galleries such as Arter (Istiklal Caddesi 211, T 212 243 3767) and SALT (Istiklal Caddesi 136, T 212 292 7605).

For a lunch break, Çağlar likes Karaköy Lokantası (Kemankeş Caddesi 37a, T 212 292 4455), a great eaterie in the dock area. In warmer weather, the terrace of Kantin (Akkavak Sokaği 30, T 212 219 3114) in Nişantaşı serves delicious seasonal vegetable dishes. After work, she favours the lively Taksim/Tünel area, where she meets friends at Asmali Cavit (Asmalimescit Caddesi 16, T 212 292 4950), a classic *meyhane* (bar/restaurant) serving raki and mezze. Later, she often calls into the upstairs bar at Münferit (see p060).

In summer, Çağlar heads up the Bosphorus for an early-morning workout or run on the promenade from Kuruçeşme to Rumeli Hisari. On the way back to Beyoğlu, she stops for a quick breakfast at Bebek Kahvesi (Cevdetpasa Caddesi 13, T 212 257 5402), a traditional tea garden in chic Bebek. For a long weekend lunch, she takes a trip to Da Mario (Dihayat Sokak 7, T 212 265 1596) in Etiler in the hills. A recommended shopping adventure is rummaging through the antique shops in Horhor (Horhor Caddesi, Tulumba Kırma Sokak) in traditional Fatih.

For full addresses, see Resources.

ARCHITOUR

A GUIDE TO ISTANBUL'S ICONIC BUILDINGS

Most of the recent large-scale architecture in Istanbul is far from the centre of the city and far from galvanising; exceptions include Santralistanbul (opposite) and the Vakko Fashion & Power Media Centre (see p066). Generally, 1980s-style 'McBuildings' define the business district and the sprawling outskirts, and a building boom across the country is leading to bland new houses being constructed at the rate of 400,000 per year.

The main focus of our architour of the last century are the works of Sedad Hakkı Eldem. Born in Turkey in 1908, Eldem studied in the West before returning to Istanbul and the Academy of Fine Arts, where he became an assistant professor in 1932. Eldem was one of the protagonists of modernist architecture in Turkey. After early flirtations with other movements, towards the end of his career he developed a recognisable personal style infused with a regional flavour. The structures we point you to include his additions to Istanbul University (see p068), Sosyal Sigortalar Külliyesi (see p013) and Atatürk Kitaplığı (see p069).

It's also worth remembering that while Ankara may have embraced modernism in an altogether purer fashion, Istanbul ironically played some part in shaping the movement, as the form of the city's great mosques and their domes influenced the developing aesthetic of Le Corbusier, who visited in 1911.

For full addresses, see Resources.

Santralistanbul

The transformation of this century-old electric power station into a centre of contemporary culture was overseen by three of the leading lights in modern Turkish architecture over the past 20 years: Nevzat Sayın, Emre Arolat and Han Tümertekin. Based at the Bilgi University campus on the upper Golden Horn, the monolithic main gallery building (above), sheathed in metal mesh and sitting on an exposed concrete base, has been called fascist architecture, but is, in fact, an elegant foil to the hodgepodge squatter neighbourhoods surrounding the site. The art galleries and nearby cafés (see p054) provide an excellent excursion into a district of Istanbul that is rapidly growing in importance.

Kazım Karabekir Caddesi 2, Eyüp,
T 212 311 7809, www.santralistanbul.org

Vakko Fashion & Power Media Centre

Set on the Asian hills of the Bosphorus, the Vakko Fashion Centre, designed by New York-based architects REX, is one of Istanbul's standout new buildings. Cem Hakko, of the venerable textile brand, gave REX's Joshua Prince-Ramus the task of completing this project in less than a year. Miraculously, a plan for an unbuilt REX structure matched the brief, allowing for a rapid progression from commission to construction that saw the building finished on time in 2010. Vakko's offices occupy the upper steel core and sleek glass-lined concrete ring; below are the Power Media offices, a public design library and galleries for Vakko's fashion collections and textiles, dating back to the 1950s.
*Kuşbakışı Caddesi 35, Nakkaştepe,
T 216 554 0700, www.vakko.com*

Istanbul University

Atatürk founded modern Istanbul University as it is today. In the 1950s, Sedad Hakkı Eldem built new faculties on Ordu Caddesi, which are not to be confused with the older campus (pictured) off Beyazıt Square, built between 1866 and 1870. With its monumental blocks, it is fundamentally fascist, softened by a pastel-pink hue and influenced by German architects such as Paul Bonatz, Bruno Taut and Clemens Holzmeister, who were busy building Ankara at the time. The 1920s observatory and Beyazıt Tower, finished in 1828, complete the university complex and its mishmash of styles.

34452 Beyazıt/Eminönü, T 212 440 0000, www.istanbul.edu.tr

Atatürk Kitaplığı
Although it's small, this library, reopened in 1976, is an excellent representation of Sedad Hakkı Eldem's later style, built as it was with ample funding and the architect's trademark overhanging eaves, tiled panels and vertically proportioned windows. It was conceived as a cultural centre with exhibition spaces and a museum, but later scaled down into a calm oasis for bookworms in the know.

Floor-to-ceiling windows exploit the view over the Bosphorus, and the upstairs reading room is lit by skylights in the ceiling domes. The building's honeycomb footprint was originally designed by Eldem for a Turkish restaurant in the Hilton Istanbul (T 212 315 6000).
Mete Caddesi 45, T 212 249 0945

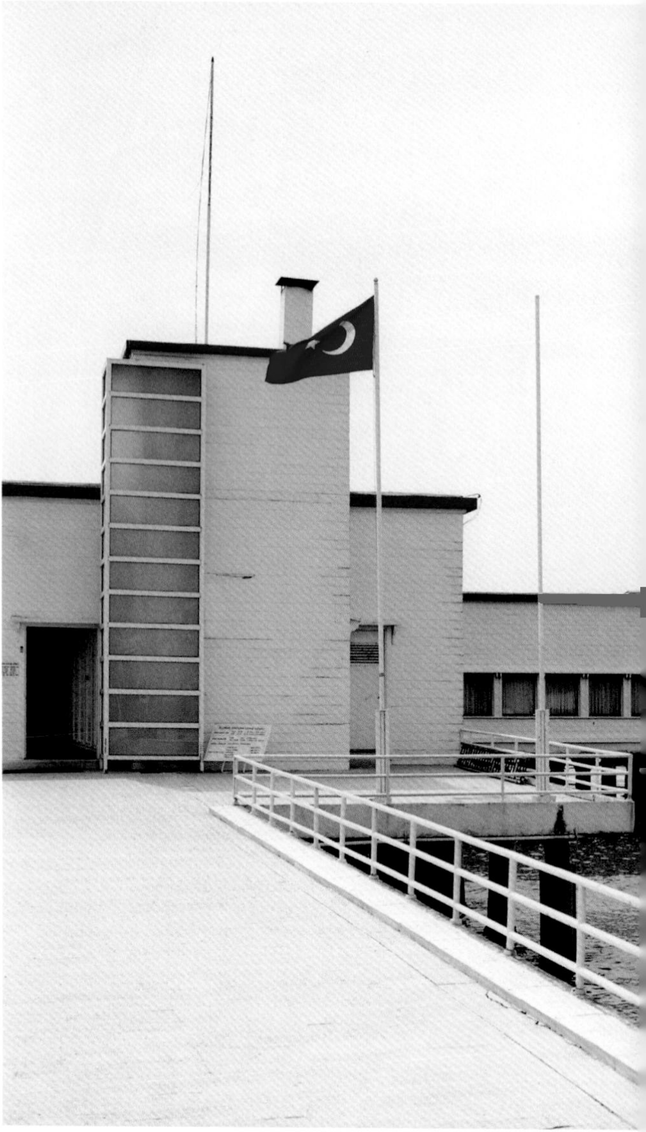

Atatürk Deniz Köskü

Constructed as a summerhouse for
Atatürk in 1935, the Marine Mansion
turned the quiet beach spot of Florya,
west of Istanbul, into a popular resort.
Edward VIII and Wallis Simpson were
among the dignitaries who stayed
here. Considering the whole thing was
constructed in a mere 43 days, it has
survived miraculously well.
Atatürk Deniz Köskü, T 212 426 5151

SHOPPING

THE BEST RETAIL THERAPY AND WHAT TO BUY

If you're a tourist, shopping in Istanbul generally means being pursued by overzealous carpet sellers near Sultanahmet – though don't miss an exception to the rule in the shape of Abdulla Natural Products (see p077), which sells handmade goods with a contemporary sensibility popular with the likes of Bryan Ferry and Catherine Deneuve. Rich Istanbulites tend to steer clear of these persistent pedlars and shop in the luxury stores around Nişantaşı or the big malls of Levent and Etiler, such as Istinye Park (Istinye Bayırı Caddesi 73, T 212 345 5555). Although the city is seeing an explosion of malls, they haven't swallowed up independent traders and shopping is still a lively pastime.

The gentrification of Çukurcuma and Cihangir gave rise to a number of antique and vintage shops, such as Christopher Hall's Hall (Faik Pasa Caddesi 6, T 212 292 9590). Then the concept store arrived. Bilstore (T 212 245 9000) sells a mix of fashion, books and homewares in branches across town, or visit Midnight Express (see p080). In a bid to rein in the ramshackle retail environment, established names have flocked to two emporiums. AddresIstanbul (Halide Edip Adivar Mallesi Sisli, T 212 320 6262) is a design hub with more than 40 stores, among them glassmaker Paşabahçe (Iş Kuleleri, Kule 3, T 212 210 9500), and the open-air Kanyon (Büyükdere Caddesi 185, T 212 353 5300) has some 160 shops over four floors. *For full addresses, see Resources.*

Derin Design Showroom

When it launched in 2004, Derin sparked an international buzz around Turkish design that has continued to this day. With more than 250 pieces to its name, the group, led by Derin Sarıye, has been building a collection since 1999 and is now Turkey's most forward-looking furniture designer. In 2009, the Derin showroom relocated to Gayrettepe. Although Derin now has distributors in many cities around the world, its Istanbul showroom is the only place you can view the entire collection, from tables and chairs to storage solutions, such as this 'Cross' unit (above), €1,245, by Aziz Sarıyer. *Hoşsohbet Sokak, Çelik Ap 20/1, T 212 274 1904, www.derindesign.com*

Yastık by Rifat Özbek

Fashion designer Rıfat Özbek — once a leading light of the catwalks of New York and London — is now designing pillow cushions. His fashion always contained a hint of his country of origin, and his designs for Yastık ('cushion' in Turkish) remix and reuse classic national patterns and motifs from ceramics and rugs with bold colours. Be warned: although they come in different shapes and sizes, it is only cushions and more cushions in this minimal white shop hidden behind the Teşvikiye Mosque, but they show off Özbek's talent in all manner of fabrics. *Şakayık Sokak 13/1, T 212 240 8731, www.yastikbyrifatozbek.com*

V2K Designers

Vakko is one of Turkey's best-known fashion houses and for several years has produced original collections of women's and men's clothes sold in its stores around town. With the V2K brand, located in the Kanyon shopping centre, the label presents its edit of the best contemporary fashion from other designers, including Hussein Chalayan, Karl Lagerfeld, Viktor & Rolf, Anna Sui and Yohji Yamamoto. This selection is complemented by sportier gear, from Ksubi, James Jeans and Superfine, aimed at a younger clientele.
Kanyon, Büyükdere Caddesi 138,
T 212 353 1080, www.vakko.com

Abdulla Natural Products

The Grand Bazaar can be a confusing jumble of Eastern bric-a-brac. Finding good-quality, well-designed items among the knock-off designer bags, tourist tat, gold jewellery and oriental carpets requires a steely eye and bargaining bravado. No such powers are required at Abdulla Natural Products. A combination of new and old design thinking by the owner and creative director Metin Tosun has resulted in a collection of first-class home textiles and linens handmade in villages throughout Turkey. Shopping here is a sensual experience as the sweet smell of olive-oil soap wafts through Abdulla's stores in the Bazaar and outside on Nurosmaniye Caddesi next door to the Fes Café (T 212 526 3071).
Alibaba Türbe Sokak 25, T 212 526 3070, www.abdulla.com

Armaggan

Modern Turkey has generally been indifferent to traditional Turkish culture. In the drive for progress, culture and craft were relegated to an inferior role. This has changed in recent years as designers have started to value historic techniques. Armaggan, a design and manufacturing brand, creates products inspired by Anatolia, the area east of Istanbul where many traditional crafts are still practised. The flagship store in Nişantaşı sells limited-edition handmade objects, such as tableware made of Diyarbakir black pearl marble lined with gold-plated silver (above), €1,680 per piece. Other smart buys include home acessories and jewellery brilliantly coloured with natural dyes.
Bostan Sokak 8, T 212 291 6292, www.armaggan.com

Midnight Express
This ironically named store, with outlets in Nişantaşı and Bebek (pictured), sells women's fashion, jewellery and design objects by international and Turkish labels. Curated by fashion designer Banu Bora and architect Tayfun Mumcu, the stock reflects a mix of popular trends and a healthy respect for tradition.
Küçük Bebek Caddesi 7a, T 212 265 4547, www.midnightexpress.com.tr

Galeri Non

It is sometimes hard to be a pioneer. Curator and gallery owner Derya Demir of Galeri Non has been at the vanguard of art that questions the cultural and political basis of Turkey. Her stable of young artists, including Extrastruggle, Nazim Hikmet Richard Dikbaş and the irreverent Esat Başak, pushes buttons on both sides of the political spectrum that have been taboo for years. Despite the risks, Demir has continued to put on successful exhibitions and encourage a generation of artists from her outpost in the scruffy district of Tophane, below Taksim. Not all the work on show is politically heavy duty. The embroideries pictured here are by Emel Kurhan, one half of jewellery and accessories design duo Yazbukey, in her first solo exhibition, 'Travelling Without Moving', in 2011.
Boğazkesen Caddesi 27a, T 212 249 8774, www.galerinon.com

A La Turca

Selling a range of wares from vintage
clothes to televisions, furniture to toys,
the area of Çukurcuma has the best
galleries and serious antique shops
in the city. Among these is A La Turca,
a converted four-storey townhouse-cum-
showroom owned by Erkal Aksoy. Opened
in 1998, it has led the way where others
in the neighbourhood have followed,
containing a treasure trove of Ottoman
and Anatolian antiques, kilims, paintings,
carpets and manuscripts, as well as a
basement full of ceramics. There is the
air of the serious collector about the place,
amplified by the lack of a name or number
on the door. Calling ahead is recommended.
Faikpaşa 4, T 212 245 2933,
www.alaturcahouse.com

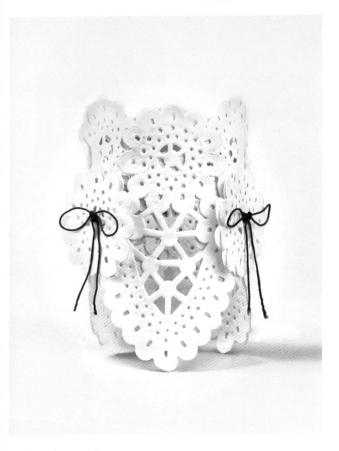

Ela Cindoruk Nazan Pak

For many years, Ela Cindoruk and Nazan Pak's extra-small jewellery shop on Atiye Sokak in Nişantaşı has been the go-to place for stylish Istanbul women who like their cosmopolitanism spiced with the old and established. Pak and Cindoruk's contemporary tastes benefit from their extensive experience of working with Istanbul's jewellery craftsmen, who are based around the Grand Bazaar. In the duo's work, the natural patina of gold and silver is shown off in simple geometries highlighted by dashes of colour. Cindoruk's series of doilies, including the 'Compass Rose' paper cuff (above), €200, reflects their traditional/modern fusion.
Atiye Sokak 14b, T 212 232 2664,
www.elacindoruknazanpak.com

Koleksiyon

Koleksiyon is one of the pioneers
of Turkey's contemporary furniture
scene, having started designing and
manufacturing its own take on the
modernist style in the mid-1970s. Led
by architect and designer Faruk Malhan,
Koleksiyon's large showroom, located
in a restored factory building in the
Bosphorus suburb of Sarıyer, is a bit
of a schlep, but worth it for its access

to original designs by Malhan and a good
collection of pieces by international
designers. Don't miss Malhan's Turkish
tea and raki glasses; ceramicist Alev
Ebuzziya's Tigris vases and Karim Rashid's
multicoloured glasswear for Gaia & Gino.
Bağlar Caddesi 35, Sarıyer, T 212 223 1320

SPORTS AND SPAS
WORK OUT, CHILL OUT OR JUST WATCH

Istanbul does not seem like a sporty city, but Istanbulites like to play (and sometimes that can involve a pair of trainers). Municipal facilities such as tennis courts, swimming pools and sports fields are few and far between, but with research and a full wallet it is possible to do almost anything. As modern metropolitan living takes hold, a plethora of gyms have opened up around Beyoğlu, along with private fitness clubs such as Hillside City Club (Alkent Sitesi Tepecik Yolu, T 212 352 2333) and MAC (Büyükdere Caddesi 185, T 212 353 0999). Joggers pound the paths of Yildiz Parkı and take to the waterside walkways alongside the Bosphorus in the morning before the fishermen and the tourists have docked.

But this is first and foremost a seafaring city, and locals make the most of the water, often for financial reasons rather than fun. Traffic on the Bosphorus is heavy, and swirling currents make it an unwelcoming place for amateur sailors, though there are plenty of opportunities for novices further upstream. In summer, locals swarm to the beaches and resorts of the Marmara and Black Seas, towels underarm and picnic baskets in hand. Off-season, the resorts, in particular Burç Beach in Kılyos, devote themselves to sailing and kitesurfing. And if you can gather your own mini football team together, it's never a problem to find both opponents and a pitch in a city that is obsessed with the sport.
For full addresses, see Resources.

Hammams

Istanbulites love visiting the local hammam. Many are crowded, display dubious levels of cleanliness and are serviced by staff who don't speak English (though they'll usually give it a good try). But don't let this stop you. They're still worth a trip, as watching locals undergo treatments, with various levels of enjoyment, in often sumptuous marble surroundings, is to witness a truly Turkish ritual. Located in what was the waterfront home of the Ottoman sultans, the Turkish Hammam (above) at the Çırağan Palace (T 212 326 4646) is – partly because of its elaborate decorations and columns – an institution in itself, as are Galatasaray Hamamı (T 212 252 4242 for men; T 212 249 4342 for women), and Çemberlitaş Hamamı (T 212 522 7974), designed by Ottoman architect Mimar Sinan.

BİR GÜN HERKES FENERBAHÇELİ OLACAK   HEP DE

Şükrü Saracoğlu Stadium

To say that football is a popular pastime in Turkey is to miss the point – it verges on a religious experience. Rivalries between Istanbul's three major clubs (Beşiktaş, Fenerbahçe and Galatasaray) are waged with a zealous devotion. Fenerbahçe's Şükrü Saracoğlu Stadium, located in Kadıköy, was renovated in 2003, and its 52,500 capacity still almost exactly matches that of Galatasaray's new Türk Telekom Arena, which opened in 2011. Matches are generally played on Friday, Saturday and Sunday nights, and you can get tickets from Biletix.com or, for those less in-demand fixtures, by rocking up to the stadium on the day.
Fenerbahçe Tesisleri, T 216 542 1907, www.fenerbahce.org

Belgrade Forest

A number of Byzantine bridges and historic aqueducts are testament to the fact that this ancient forest, 40 minutes north of Istanbul by car, was once the source of an expansive water supply system under the Ottomans. At weekends in summer, locals come to the fringes of the woods to picnic and cook up kebabs by the side of their cars, but once you're inside the forest it is possible to escape from everyone. Weaving through the trees is a 6.5km running and cycling circuit with 17 fitness points and suggestions for various exercises. If you prefer an off-piste adventure, there are plenty of tucked-away Byzantine remains to explore.

Caudalie Vinotherapie Spa
Since opening in 2006, Les Ottomans
Hotel has been known for its fastidious
attention to the details of luxury and
comfort. This extended to Turkey's first
vinotherapy spa, open to non-guests,
on the ground floor of the Bosphorus
yalı. Try the grape-pulp skin treatment,
part of its numerous hammam therapies.
*Muallim Naci Caddesi 68, T 212 359 1500,
www.lesottomans.com*

ESCAPES

WHERE TO GO IF YOU WANT TO LEAVE TOWN

While you're in Istanbul, do as the locals do and exit the city, at least for a day or two. There's plenty to do, from exploring the surreal landscape of Cappadocia (see p098) to lounging on the beaches of the European side of the Bosphorus or on the Black Sea coast. Here you'll find villages such as Ağva and Polonezköy, a Polish settlement dating back to the 1840s, which make for great day or weekend trips. In summer, resorts such as Şile and Kılyos offer fishing, swimming and canoeing. Crossing the Black Sea to Ukraine, Yalta (opposite) offers an interesting change of pace. On the eastern coast, the Russian resort of Sochi is a destination with a glamour factor that will increase in the build-up to the Winter Olympics, to be held there in 2014. If you're visiting now, stay at Grand Hotel Rodina (Ulitsa Vinogradnaya 33, T +7 8622 539 000).

South of Istanbul, ancient Bursa and neighbouring spa town Çekirge are worth a visit. Closer to the city, Princes' Islands (see p102) are peppered with restaurants and Ottoman-style houses, and populated by faded aristocrats, Armenian gold dealers and all manner of eccentrics. If you'd like longer on the water, book a Blue Voyage (www.bluevoyage.com), for a cruise in a wide-keeled gulet to the most beautiful coves on Turkey's Aegean and Mediterranean coasts. These trips began when Istanbul artists roughed it on fishing boats. Not any more – now these crafts are like boutique hotels. *For full addresses, see Resources.*

Yalta, Ukraine

The Crimean peninsula is just two hours away from Istanbul by turboprop. Ever since Catherine the Great decided this coast would make a useful addition to her empire, the shores around Yalta have been dotted with dachas designed to take in the invigorating breezes. The likes of Pushkin, Gorky and Chekhov composed key works here, and Chekhov died here (his cottage remains a local shrine). We recommend a tour of the Stalinist architecture that dots the coast, such as the former Friendship Hotel (above) near Yalta, in Artek. If you want to overnight, check into Hotel Yalta (T +38 654 270 260) or the landmark Hotel Oreanda (T +38 654 274 250).

Cappadocia

Scoured by wind and water, the landscape of Central Anatolia has a moon-like quality, with its 'fairy chimneys' – cone-shaped pillars of volcanic rock – and endless mazes of caves, passageways and churches dug into the hills by early Christians. A one-hour flight from Istanbul to Kayseri or Nevşehir, followed by up to an hour's drive, brings you to the town of Ürgüp.

Our favourite lodging is the Serinn hotel (pictured), a beautifully restored property, where the interiors (overleaf), by Rıfat Ergör, mix modern furnishings with the rough beauty of the rock. Take a balloon ride or wander the hills, then watch the sun set from the terrace with some of the region's earthy red wine. *Esbelli Sokak 36, Ürgüp, Cappadocia, T 384 341 6076, www.serinnhouse.com*

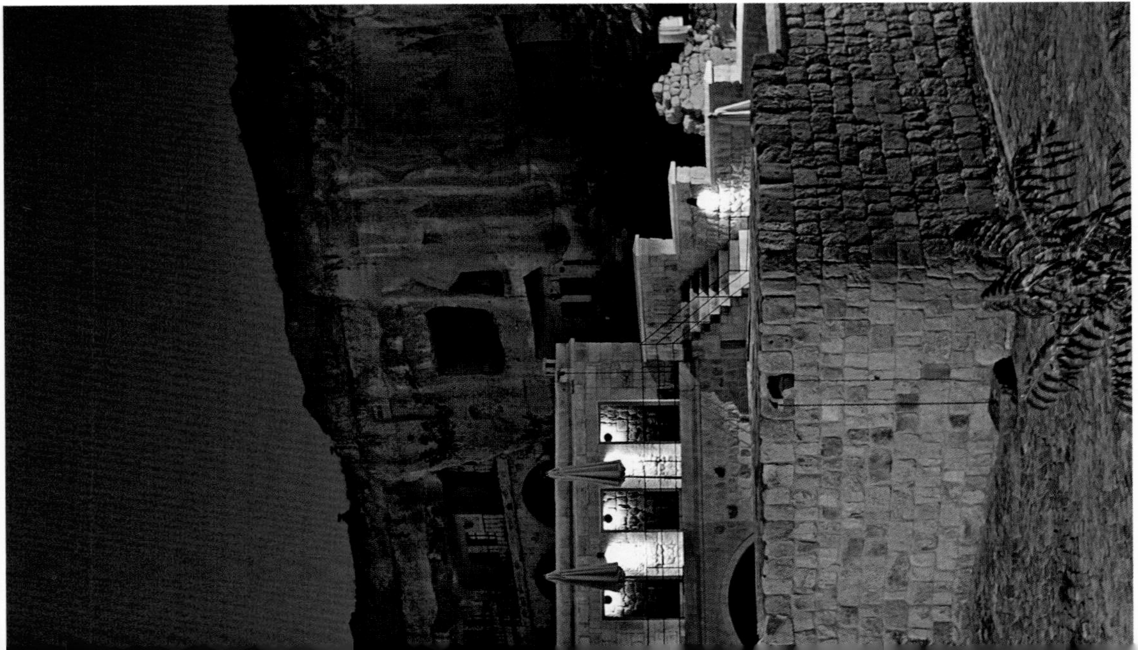

Room 5, Serinn House

Princes' Islands
For a great view of the city, nothing
beats this 90-minute boat trip across
the Marmara Sea. There are nine
traffic-free islands in the chain, the
closest of which is windswept Kınalıada,
home to a large Armenian population.
The ferry also stops at Heybelıada
(pictured), partly a naval base, before
making its way to the jewel in the
crown, Büyükada, the largest island.

NOTES
SKETCHES AND MEMOS

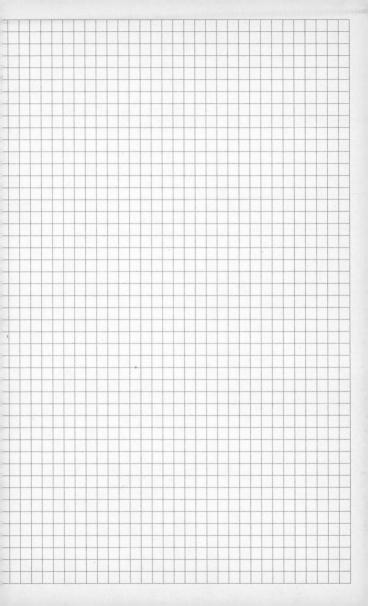

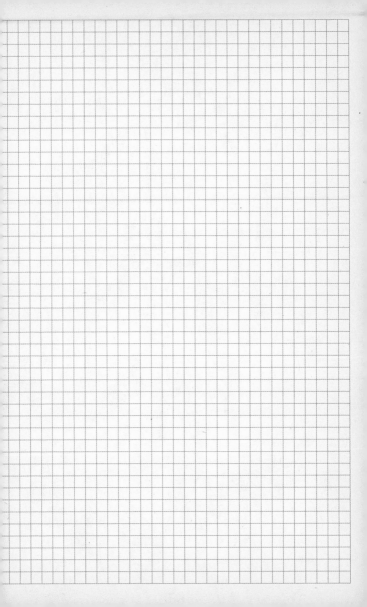

RESOURCES

CITY GUIDE DIRECTORY

HOTELS

ADDRESSES AND ROOM RATES

A'jia 022
Room rates:
double, from €190;
Bosphorous Pasha Room, from €860
Çubuklu Caddesi 27
T 216 413 9300
www.ajiahotel.com

Bentley Hotel 016
Room rates:
double, from €380
Halaskargazi Caddesi 75
T 212 291 7730
www.bentley-hotel.com

Çırağan Palace Kempinski 016
Room rates:
double, from €510
Çırağan Caddesi 32
T 212 326 4646
www.kempinski.com

The Istanbul Edition 016
Room rates:
double, from €245
Büyükdere Casdesi 136/1
T 212 317 7700
www.editionhotels.com

Four Seasons Hotel Bosphorus 020
Room rates:
double, from €520;
Palace Bosphorus Room, from €1,460
Çırağan Caddesi 28,
T 212 381 4000
www.fourseasons.com/bosphorus

Four Seasons Hotel Sultanahmet 016
Room rates:
double, from €490
Tevkifhane Sokak 1,
T 212 402 3000
www.fourseasons.com/istanbul

Grand Hotel Rodina 096
Room rates:
double, from €415
Ulitsa Vinogradnaya 33
Sochi
Russia
T +7 8622 539 000
www.grandhotelrodina.ru

The House Hotel Bosphorous 028
Room rates:
double, from €229
Salhane Sok 1
T 212 244 3400
www.thehousehotel.com

The House Hotel Galatasaray 028
Room rates:
double, from €149
Firuzaga Mahallesi Bostanbası 19
T 212 244 3400
www.thehousehotel.com

The House Hotel Nişantaşı 028
Room rates:
double, from €129;
Terrace Deluxe Room, from €199
Abdi Ipekci Caddesi 34
T 212 224 5999
www.thehousehotel.com

Hotel Oreanda 097
Room rates:
double, from €210
35/2 Lenina Street
Yalta
Ukraine
T +38 654 274 250
www.hotel-oreanda.com

Serinn House 098
  Room rates:
  double, from €100;
  Room 5, €115
  Esbelli Sokak 36
  Ürgüp
  Cappadocia
  T 384 341 6076
  www.serinnhouse.com
The Sofa Hotel 030
  Room rates:
  double, €170;
  Executive Suite, €800
  Teşvikiye Caddesi 41
  T 212 368 1818
  www.thesofahotel.com
Sumahan on the Water 026
  Room rates:
  double, €145;
  Executive Suite, from €425
  Kuleli Caddesi 51
  T 216 422 8000
  www.sumahan.com
Tomtom Suites 016
  Room rates:
  double, from €169
  Boğazkesen Caddesi 18
  T 212 292 4949
  www.tomtomsuites.com
W 024
  Room rates:
  double, from €250;
  Wow Suite, from €3,560
  Süleyman Seba Caddesi 22
  T 212 381 2121
  www.winstanbul.com.tr

Witt 017
  Room rates:
  double, from €179;
  City View Suite, €229;
  Penthouse Suite, €389
  Defterdar Yokusu 26
  T 212 293 1500
  www.wittistanbul.com
Hotel Yalta 097
  Room rates:
  double, from €50
  50 Drazhinsky Street
  Yalta
  Ukraine
  T +38 654 270 260
  www.hotel-yalta.com

WALLPAPER* CITY GUIDES

Executive Editor
Rachael Moloney

Authors
Gökhan Karakus
Emma O'Kelly

Art Director
Loran Stosskopf

Art Editor
Eriko Shimazaki
Designer
Lara Collins
Map Illustrator
Russell Bell

Photography Editor
Sophie Corben
Deputy Photography Editor
Anika Burgess
Photography Assistant
Nabil Butt

Senior Sub-Editor
Nick Mee
Sub-Editors
Vanessa Harriss
Greg Hughes

Editorial Assistant
Emma Harrison
Intern
Ayse Koklu

**Wallpaper* Group
Editor-in-Chief**
Tony Chambers
Publishing Director
Gord Ray
Managing Editor
Jessica Diamond

Contributor
Murat Tufan

Wallpaper* ® is a
registered trademark
of IPC Media Limited

First published 2006
Second edition (revised
and updated) 2008
Third edition (revised
and updated) 2011
© 2006, 2008 and 2011
IPC Media Limited

ISBN 978 0 7148 6269 9

PHAIDON

Phaidon Press Limited
Regent's Wharf
All Saints Street
London N1 9PA

Phaidon Press Inc
180 Varick Street
New York, NY 10014

Phaidon® is a registered
trademark of Phaidon
Press Limited

www.phaidon.com

A CIP Catalogue record for
this book is available from
the British Library.

All prices are correct at
the time of going to press,
but are subject to change.

Printed in China

PHOTOGRAPHERS

ISTANBUL
A COLOUR-CODED GUIDE TO THE HOT 'HOODS

EMINÖNÜ/CAĞALOĞLU
A fascinating and frenetic introduction to the city, this area is a ceaseless hive of activity

ÜSKÜDAR/KADIKÖY
The Asiatic origins of Istanbul are on display everywhere in these traditional quarters

TÜNEL/KARAKÖY
The docks are no longer sin central. Visit the Istanbul Modern for a contemporary art fix

SULTANAHMET
The numerous sights here are not to be missed. Just beware the numerous salesmen

ÇUKURCUMA/CIHANGIR
The buzzy, café-lined centre of the new bohemian city is more Soho than Stamboul

BEYOĞLU/TAKSIM
Istanbul's heartland is getting smarter, smoother and, sadly, a little staler by the day

ORTAKÖY/BEŞIKTAŞ
These Bosphorus-side 'burbs are the place to take in some local culture and have fun

NIŞANTAŞI/MAÇKA
Sleek boutiques and arty ateliers are replacing the souks in these upscale districts

For a full description of each neighbourhood, see the Introduction.
Featured venues are colour-coded, according to the district in which they are located.